Monet

THE ESSENTIAL PAINTINGS

Monet

THE ESSENTIAL PAINTINGS

Anne Sefrioui

PRESTEL
MUNICH • LONDON • NEW YORK

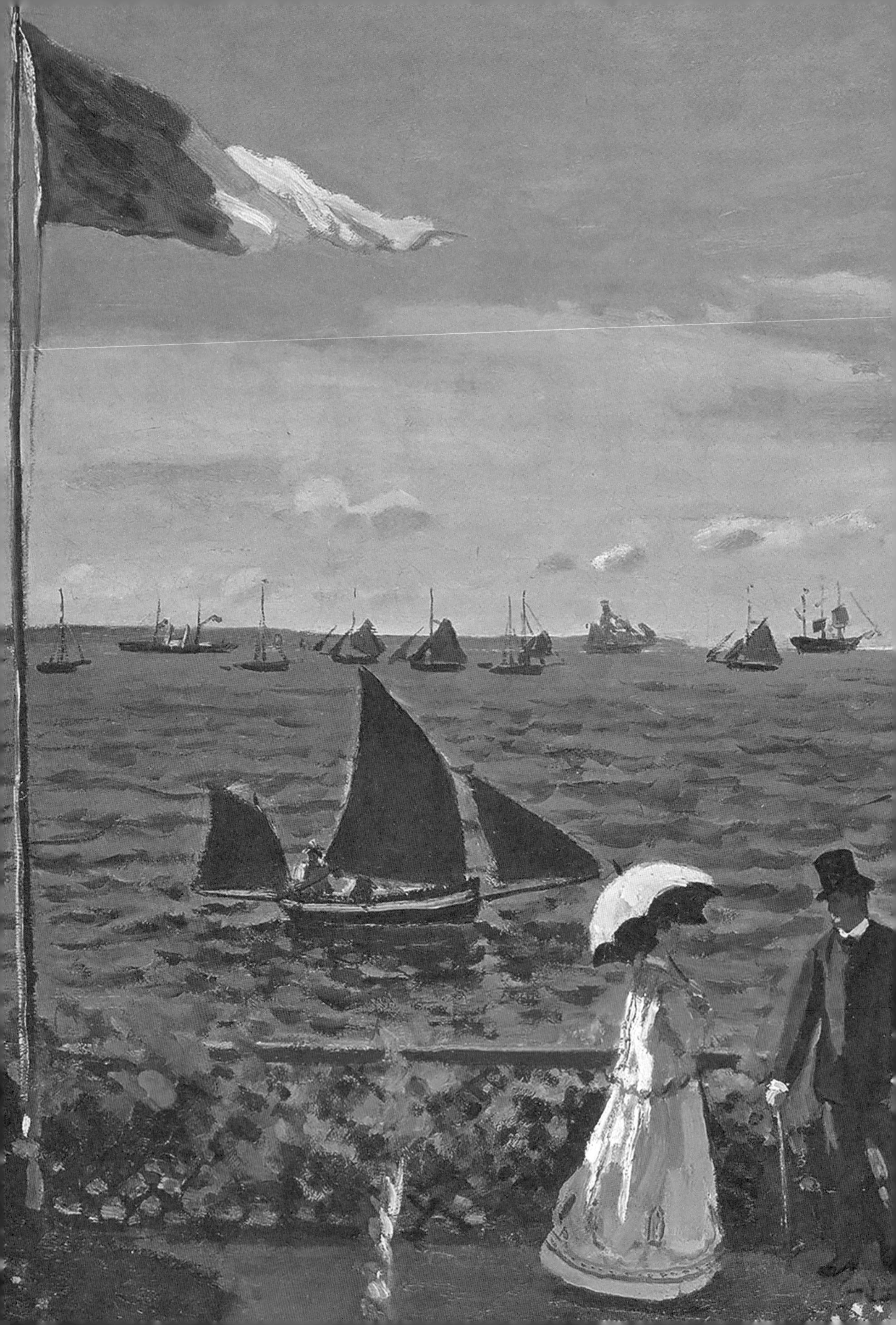

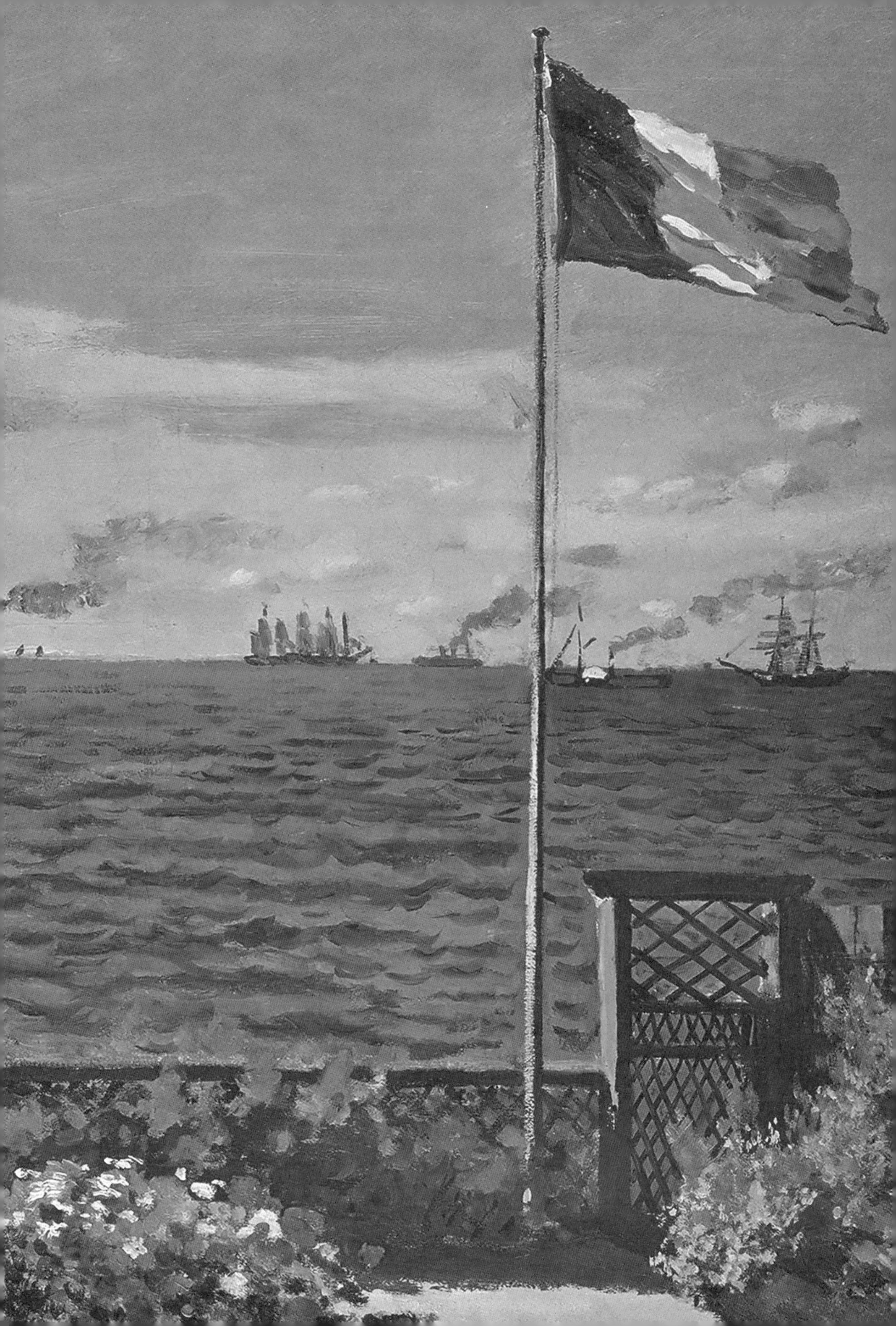

The "Raphael of Water" – such was the nickname given to Claude Monet, as the liquid element, omnipresent throughout his paintings, is captured with rare virtuosity. From the calm or violent seas of the Normandy coast to the warmth of the Mediterranean shores, from the shimmering river Seine to the misty ponds and water lily basins, throughout his career, the artist never ceased to render the fluid reality of water, constantly altering his technique, always in search of the most accurate expression of his feelings. For over sixty years, Monet mainly committed to this theme, developing a body of work that first bore the hallmark of realism in the 1860s, then embodied Impressionism in its purest form. He then established himself, in the beginning of the 20th century, as one of the founders of modern art. This is the fruitful journey that this collection welcomes you to browse, presenting fifty key works that mark its stages.

This passion for water, an element central to the artist's work, may draw its roots from his personal history. Indeed, this young Parisian, born in 1840, moved to Le Havre with his family when he was five, and would spend his youth by the sea, under the changing skies of Normandy, running along the clifftops or playing on the beaches. He very likely retained some indelible feelings of these times. It was also here that, just after his teenage years, the young Oscar-Claude, who proved to have a gift for drawing, learned to set up his easel outdoors, where he practised with the painter Eugène Boudin, who gave him this advice: "Study, learn to see, and learn to paint, practise your landscapes." "If I became a painter, I owe it to Eugène Boudin," Monet would later say. Another decisive event occurred in 1862, when he met Johan Barthold Jongkind, who had travelled to Normandy to paint. A friendship would soon bind the twenty-two-year-old artist and the Dutch painter, whom he regarded as his master. "It is to him that I owe the definitive education of my eye," he would later claim.

While both these encounters would prove important, Monet also rubbed shoulders with the Parisian world of arts, and was able to observe the trends of his time. While academicism was still alive and well, and the great mythological or historical subjects still proved successful at the Salon, what drew the attention of the twenty-year-old were the paintings of landscape painters such as Constant Troyon, Charles-François Daubigny, Camille Corot and Théodore Rousseau – those whom the history of art has gathered under the moniker of the "Barbizon school of painters," and who would paint in the forest of Fontainebleau. With Camille Pissarro, whom Monet met at the Swiss Academy in 1860, then with his friends from Gleyre's atelier (Frédéric Bazille, Auguste Renoir and Alfred Sisley), who often gathered with other artists, including Édouard Manet, at the Café Guerbois, discussions were passionate, but they all agreed on the need to modernise the art of landscape painting and to paint nature on location, rather than in the studio.

This is how Claude Monet, from 1863 to 1865, in turn painted in the forest of Fontainebleau. Inspired by his elders, he adopted their green and brown palette, linear perspective, and realistic technique. In the spring of 1865, he embarked on an ambitious project: to paint a *Luncheon on the Grass* featuring life-size figures, outdoors, in the format of a historical painting. The adventure lasted one year, during which time Monet produced a considerable number of nature studies. The monumental painting (no. 1) would never be completed, but day by day, the painter refined his palette, which grew clearer and increasingly personal.

Nature had now become Monet's studio of choice, as he continuously travelled back and forth between Paris and Normandy: whether in the countryside, in gardens (no. 2) or on the seashore (no. 5), he observed the faintest changes, the variations in colour and light according to the seasons or the time of day. Snow, in particular, would become a recurring motif in the second half of the 1860s (no. 3), as would the banks of the river Seine, when, after settling near Bougival, he painted *Bain à la Grenouillère* (no. 4) working beside Renoir, multiplying technical innovations such as the broken brushstroke, which would become a cornerstone of Impressionism.

Although Monet considered life as an artist to be an exciting challenge, it also had its material drawbacks: his paintings hardly sold at the time, and his family, who disapproved of his marital life with his model, Camille Doncieux, refused to support him. The situation worsened with the War of 1870, which forced him to leave for London – an exile shared with his friend Camille Pissarro, during which a decisive encounter would, however, occur: he was introduced to the merchant Paul Durand-Ruel, who took an interest in his work and would support him by purchasing his works throughout his career.

Upon returning to France, Monet resided in Rouen and Le Havre, which allowed him to reunite with his favourite themes: the seaside (no. 6) and, above all, the banks of the river Seine, with its sailing boats and regattas. These would grow all the more accessible to him since, at the end of 1871, he settled in Argenteuil, in a house with a garden that he painted multiple times (nos. 8 and 9). The silhouettes of Camille Doncieux and their son Jean frequently appear in these works, as they do in the views of the surrounding countryside (nos. 11 and 12). It was also in the early 1870s that he set up his studio boat (no. 15), not far from his home, which allowed him to literally immerse himself in his motif.

However hard he worked, success still shunned him, as it did his comrades who sought to break free from the traditional paths of painting. Therefore, in 1874, under the name of "Société anonyme coopérative des artistes peintres, sculpteurs, graveurs et lithographes," they decided to organise an exhibition outside the Salon, where many artists had been rejected. The setting for this exhibition would be the former studio of the photographer Nadar, on the Boulevard des Capucines. Some of these artists, such as Edgar Degas or Édouard Manet, already enjoyed a certain degree of fame, but most were unknown to the general public. Monet took part in the event, presenting several paintings, including *Impression, Sunrise* (no. 13) – a title that was derided by a critic, who described these painters as "impressionists." They appropriated the word, giving rise to a movement of which Monet would undoubtedly

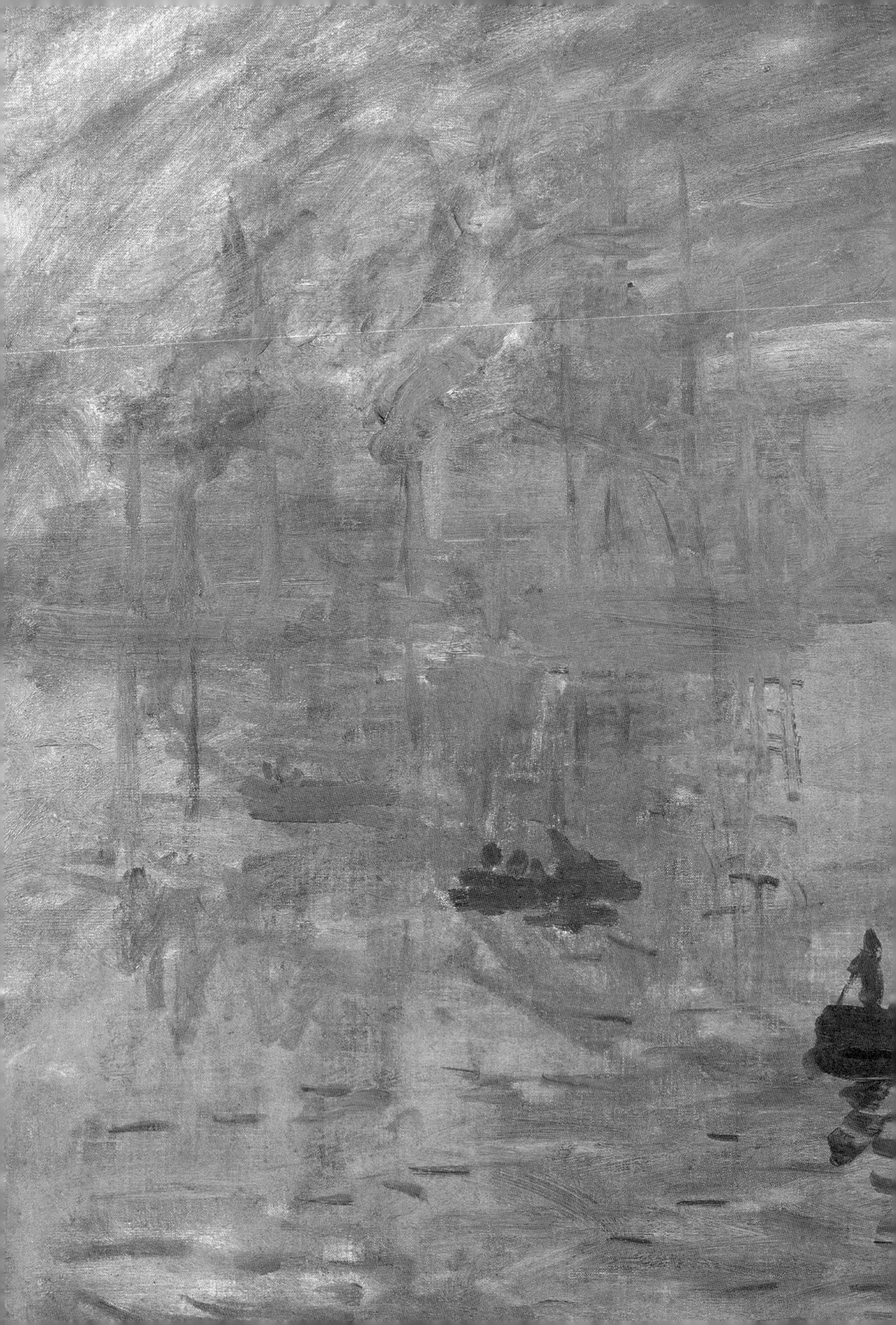

be the most perfect representative. However, the hostility or indifference of the early days would turn from a scandal into a success, as Impressionism gradually convinced and found an audience. What confused the first onlookers, who were accustomed to the smoothness of the paint and the predominance of the drawing, was the application of small, rapid and numerous brushstrokes to the canvas, to the point where distance became necessary to reconstruct the motif. The aim of the impressionists' technique was to recreate the vibration of light without resorting to the traditional chiaroscuro. Indeed, these artists considered that in nature, no colour or form exists independently of light – the same light that reflects colours and forms in changing ways, dissolving outlines. They therefore tried to translate ephemeral phenomena into paintings, setting free the famous "sensations" that Monet himself sought throughout his entire life. The artist's special relationship with nature did not prevent him from gazing at the contemporary world, witnessing its swift industrialisation at the expense of rural life. The numerous representations of the two bridges of Argenteuil (no. 14), in particular, demonstrate the painter's interest in modernity, which blossomed into the extraordinary series of views of the Gare Saint-Lazare railway station in 1877 (no. 17). The following year, he painted the French National Day in the streets of Paris, producing two canvases filled with vibrant colour and light (nos. 18 and 19): these would be his farewell to the capital, which he never painted again.

The diversity of subjects is combined with a variety of techniques; indeed, Monet does not approach a motif with a preconceived notion, but rather works with the location's particularities and atmospheric conditions. Some works, such as *The Argenteuil Bridge* (no. 14), are meticulously painted, while others, such as *Impression, Sunrise* (no. 13) display more vivid brushwork, the overall effect taking precedence over the details. However, this artist's objectives remained consistent, as he sought to convey his immediate perceptions and subjectivity, which embodied the foundation of the Impressionist aesthetic. The increasing use of colour thus allowed him to suggest forms in space, to the detriment of lines and modelling.

Relying on these principles, Monet worked relentlessly, regardless of the ups and downs of his personal life, until the early 1880s. Indeed, events would follow one another: meeting one of his collectors, Ernest Hoschedé who, in 1878, invited him to share a house in Vétheuil, reuniting both their families; the passing of Camille

Doncieux, the following year, and the complex family situation that ensued and, finally, life with Alice Hoschedé in Giverny, from 1883. During this time, his career gained momentum: he was accepted at the Salon, a personal exhibition was devoted to him in 1880, preceding the presentation of some forty works in New York in 1886, organised by Durand-Ruel.

Although Monet's following was growing, and he was finally beginning to earn a living with his paintings, he continued to pursue his obsessions as an artist: in the early 1880s, he tirelessly worked on the same subjects, particularly the Seine (nos. 20 and 22) or the coast of Normandy in changing light (nos. 23 to 26). During this period, he also travelled twice to Italy (no. 27) and sojourned on Belle-Île, which inspired him to produce some striking paintings (no. 28).

Towards the end of the decade, the painter systematised his research around the same motif, and created the principle of series of works: starting with *Haystacks* (no. 33), they continued with *Poplars* (nos. 31 and 32), *Cathedrals* (nos. 37 and 38), and *Mornings on the Seine* (no. 34). Lastly, in the 1890s, after the landscaping of his garden in Giverny (nos. 41 and 42) and the excavation works of the "water garden," water lilies would provide Monet him a new theme (nos. 43 to 47), which would become almost obsessive for thirty years, and inspire his most innovative works (nos. 48 to 50). Despite gradually losing his sight from 1910 onwards, the artist embarked on what would become the apotheosis of his body of work: the creation of an immense mural decoration, which would find its place in the two rooms of the Musée de l'Orangerie.

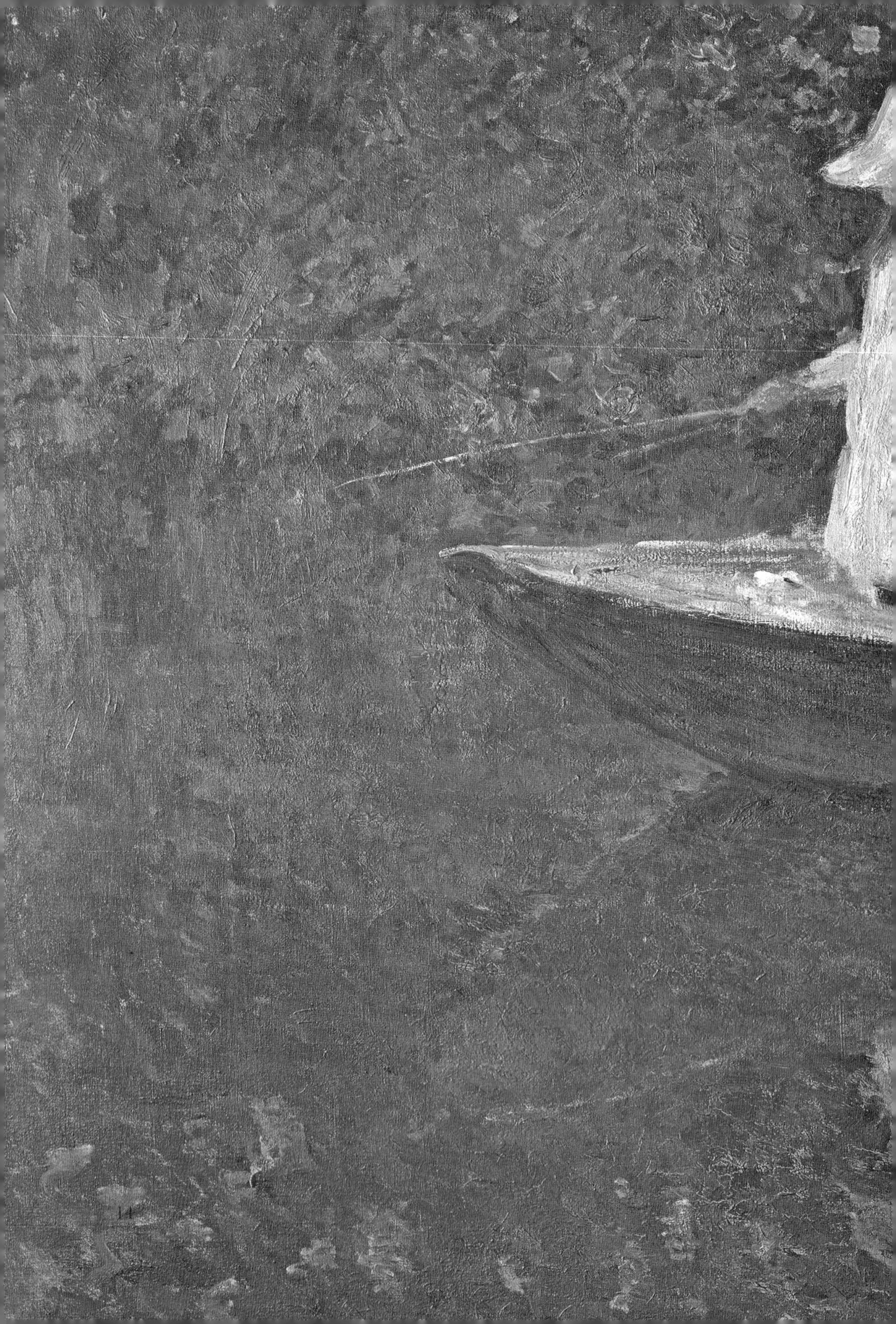

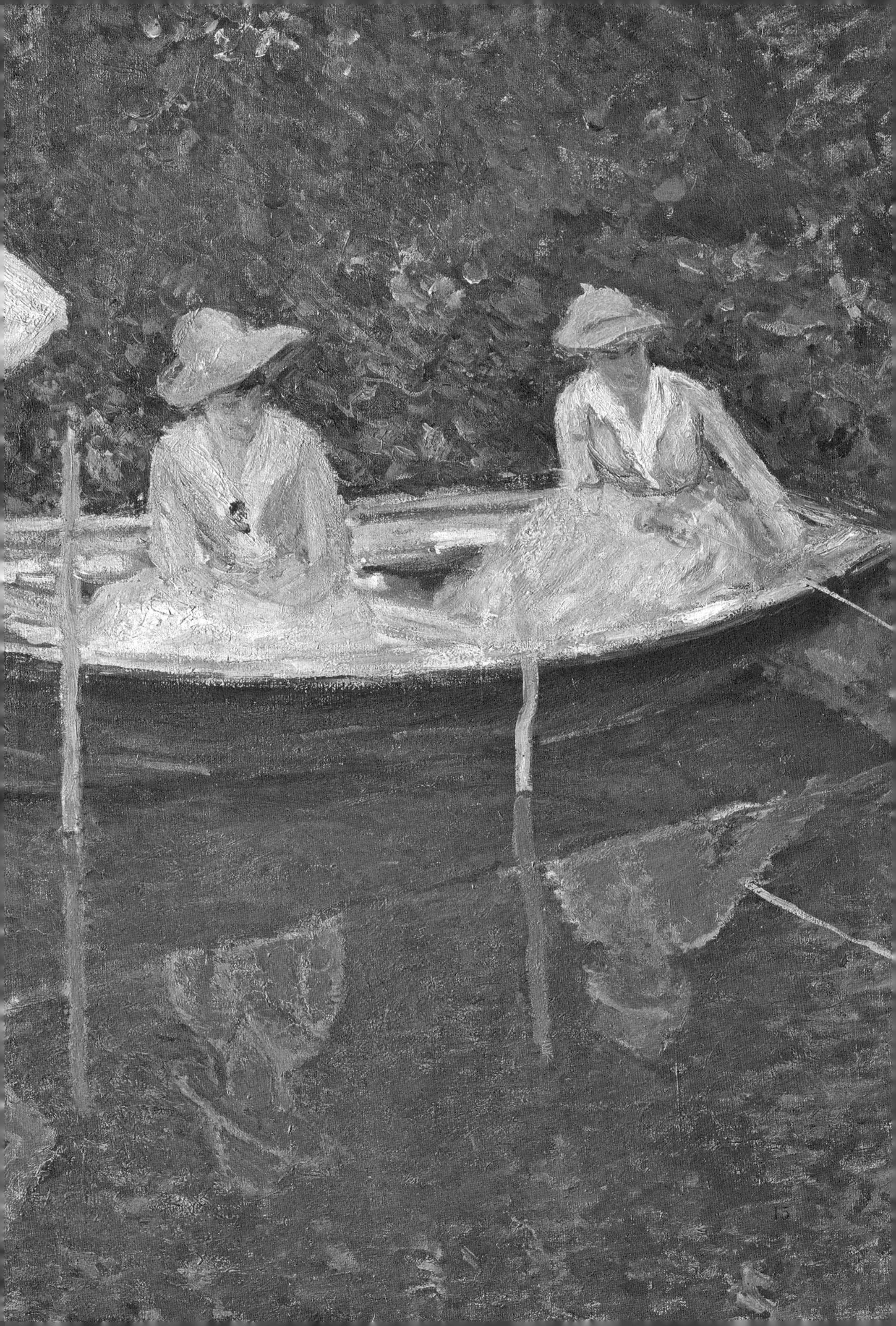

1 | *Luncheon on the Grass*

This painting is a preparatory study for the huge composition (4.60 × 6 metres) that Monet planned to present at the 1866 Salon, which would, however, never be completed. Contrary to the usual practice of sketching on location, before finishing the painting in the studio, the artist painted outdoors, in the forest of Fontainebleau, using natural light. He asked his painter friends, including Frédéric Bazille and Gustave Courbet, to pose for him, as well as Camille Doncieux, his spouse, who would be his female model in various attitudes.

2 | *Woman in the Garden*

This garden offers a very wide range of nuances of green, with densities varying according to shadows and light. After the Fontainebleau period, during which Monet worked in rather dark tones, his palette became lighter, as he began a quest for light that he would pursue throughout his life. The woman dressed in white is his aunt, an amateur painter herself, who would greatly support his early career.

3 | *The Magpie*

In the second half of the 1860s, Monet would repeatedly try his hand at the theme of snow-covered landscapes; this particular landscape was painted in the region of Étretat. This was an opportunity for him to study the variations in light, to play with nuances by using a limited number of hues: browns and blues, applied in multiple tones to add reflections to the snow, instead of representing it as a uniformly white mantle. The little magpie seems to be sitting on the fence, as if on a stave.

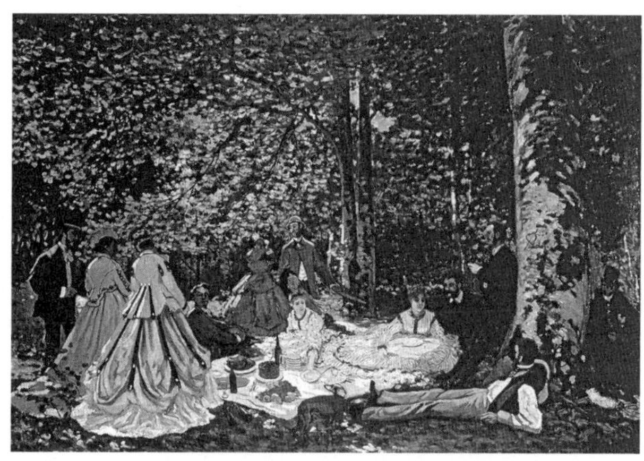

Luncheon on the Grass, 1866
Oil on canvas, 130 × 181 cm
Moscow, The Pushkin State Museum of Fine Arts

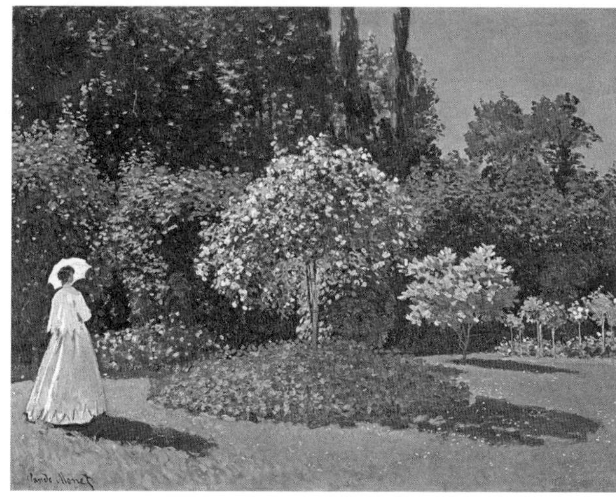

Woman in the garden, 1867
Oil on canvas, 82 × 101 cm
Saint Petersburg, State Hermitage Museum

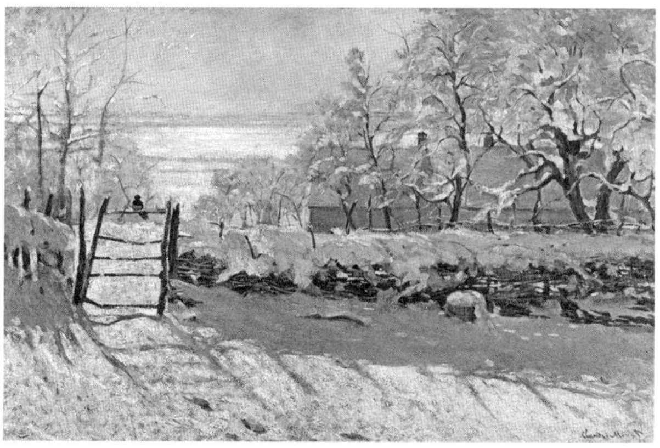

The Magpie, 1868–1869
Oil on canvas, 89 × 130 cm
Paris, Musée d'Orsay

4 | *Bain à la Grenouillère*

Having settled near Bougival, Monet often worked with Renoir, who lived nearby. Both artists repeatedly painted the Grenouillère in Bougival, a bathing establishment and floating café, where people also came to practise canoeing. This location attracted large numbers of Parisians on Sundays. While Renoir sought to suggest the atmosphere of the place, Monet was mainly concerned with reproducing the shimmer of the water and its variations, painting small horizontal rectangular patches of different colours. The painter's technique evolved: it was at this time that he experimented with the broken brushstroke.

5 | *Garden at Sainte-Adresse*

On this terrace, Monet depicted several members of his family, including his father, seated in the foreground. Everything is reminiscent of summer pleasures – flowers in full bloom, light-coloured dresses, parasols –, and one can even feel a breeze waving the flags and billowing in the sails of the boats. During his stay in Normandy, the painter would produce a number of views of the sea and beaches, while honing his technique. In paintings of this period, particularly in this one, highly fragmented brushstrokes appear in places, marking an evolution from the paintings produced in Fontainebleau two years earlier.

6 | *The Beach at Trouville*

Under a pale, luminous sky, typical of the coast of Normandy, Monet's spouse Camille and her cousin pose, sitting on the sand. The colour palette is limited, and the dresses, with their broad blue stripes on a white background, are depicted rather crudely, as the artist's aim is not to describe but to suggest, thus announcing impressionism. Similarly, the summer vacationers in the background are rendered with just a few swift brushstrokes, leaving the viewer's eye to complete the vision.

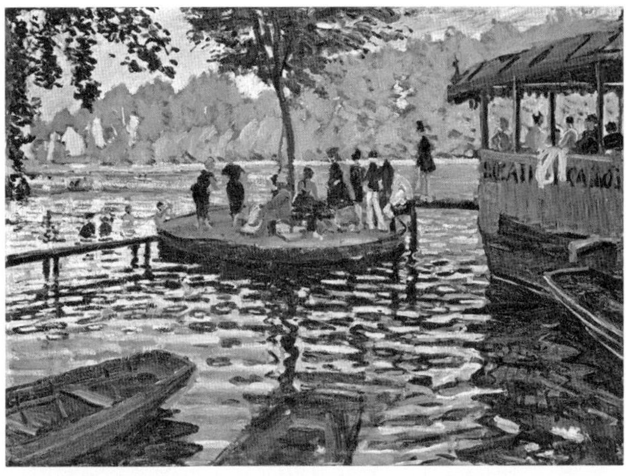

Bain à la Grenouillère, 1869
Oil on canvas, 74.6 × 99.7 cm,
New York, The Metropolitan
Museum of Art

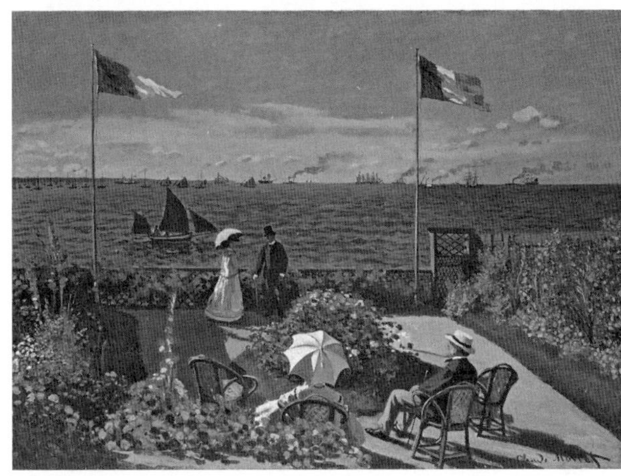

Garden in Sainte-Adresse, 1867
Oil on canvas, 98 × 130 cm,
New York, The Metropolitan
Museum of Art

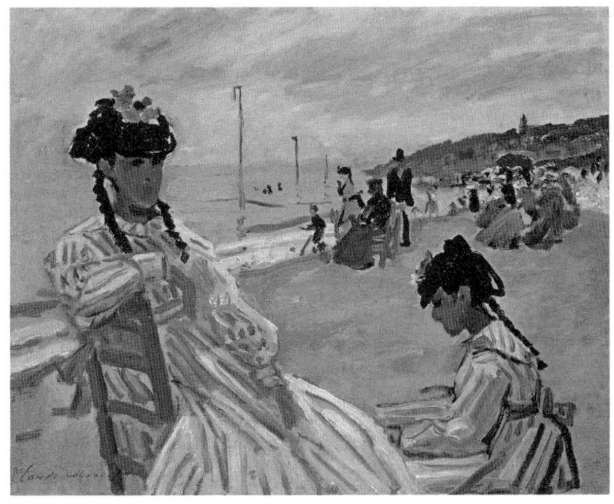

The beach at Trouville, 1870
Oil on canvas, 38 × 46 cm
Paris, Musée Marmottan Monet

7 | *Springtime*

At the end of 1871, Monet moved to Argenteuil, which was easily accessible from Paris by rail. The garden surrounding the house is the setting for many of the paintings of this period, and Monet's spouse Camille is depicted here. All of Monet's attention was focused on the patches of sunlight filtering through the foliage, illuminating the white coat and the surrounding grass.

8 | *The Artist's House at Argenteuil*

"I perhaps owe having become a painter to flowers," said Claude Monet. His garden in Argenteuil is a superb illustration of this passion. This painting features Jean, Monet's eldest son, aged five or six, while Camille, his spouse, appears in the doorway of their beautiful bourgeois home. An atmosphere of placid happiness emanates from this painting – Monet was indeed going through a prosperous period at the time, thanks to the recent acquisitions by the art dealer Paul Durand-Ruel.

9 | *The Lunch: decorative panel*

After 1870, Monet ceased producing the large formats of his early work, but a few works provided exceptions to this, including this painting presented at the second Impressionist exhibition in 1876. This painting's charm owes much to the simplicity of its subject: a family moment, the after-lunch, suggested by a table that has not yet been cleared (a pretext to paint a superb still life), by a hat hanging on a branch and by an umbrella that appears to have been left behind. Under the cool shade, little Jean plays quietly, while the sun floods the flowerbeds between which two elegant women are strolling.

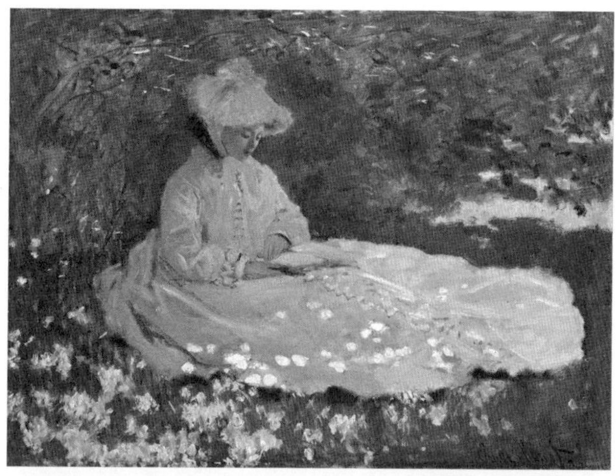

Springtime, 1872
Oil on canvas, 50 × 65.5 cm
Baltimore, The Walters Art Museum

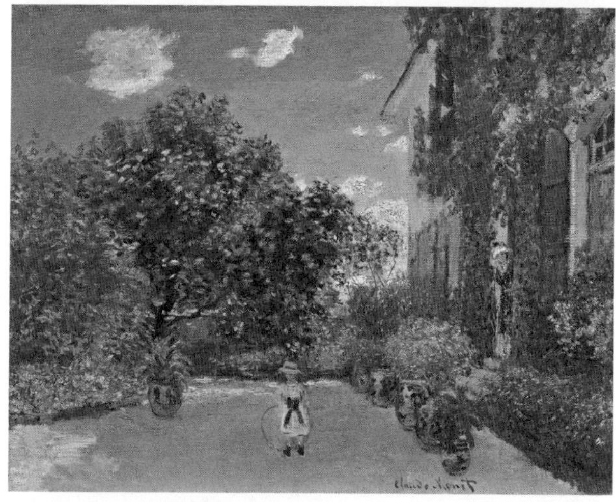

The Artist's House at Argenteuil, 1873
Oil on canvas, 60.2 × 73.3 cm
Chicago, The Art Institute

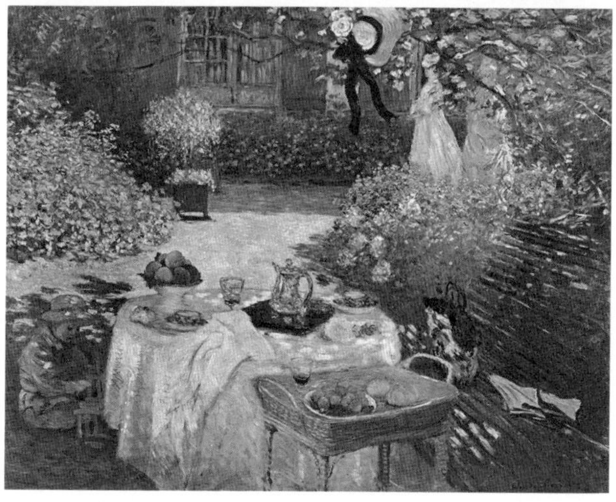

The Lunch: decorative panel, ca. 1874
Oil on canvas, 160 × 201 cm
Paris, Musée d'Orsay

10 | *Still Life with Melon*

Still life is not a genre with which one spontaneously associates Monet's name, yet the artist displayed great virtuosity from the very beginning, as evidenced by the foreground of Luncheon on the Grass (no. 1) or the table of The Lunch (no. 9). Until 1880, he would paint a few canvases on the topic of the "silent life," including in his house in Argenteuil, where he painted this melon and these peaches placed in Chinese porcelain dishes, next to this admirable bunch of grapes placed on the white tablecloth. This refinement, which was entirely in keeping with the artist's taste, would fully blossom fifteen years later, in Giverny.

11 | *Poppy Field*

Presented at the first exhibition of the Impressionist group, this painting would become one of the movement's most iconic works. It evokes the vibrant atmosphere of a stroll through the fields on a beautiful summer day. The painter diluted the contours and built a colourful rhythm using red patches that suggest rural flowers. Their oversized format in the foreground shows the primacy given to the visual impression and, in a way, prepares the path to abstraction.

12 | *Taking a Walk near Argenteuil*

During his exile in London in 1870–1871, Monet had been very impressed by the discovery of Joseph Mallord William Turner's paintings and their vaporous luminosity. He would, in his turn, use a blurred style to more accurately suggest the impermanence of natural phenomena, such as the sky, borne to life by clouds, or the field strewn with indistinct flowers, while the young woman's white dress hints at the windy atmosphere.

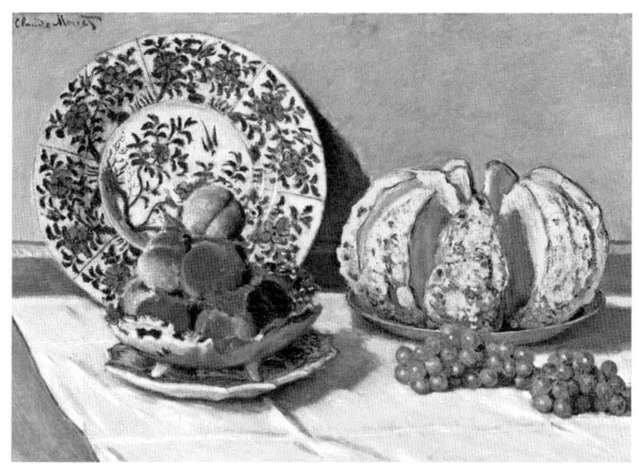

Still Life with Melon, 1872
Oil on canvas, 53 × 73 cm
Lisbon, Museu Calouste Gulbenkian

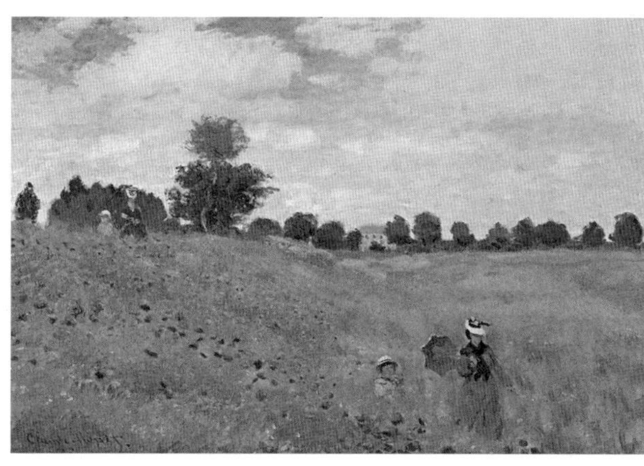

Poppy Field, 1873
Oil on canvas, 50 × 65 cm
Paris, Musée d'Orsay

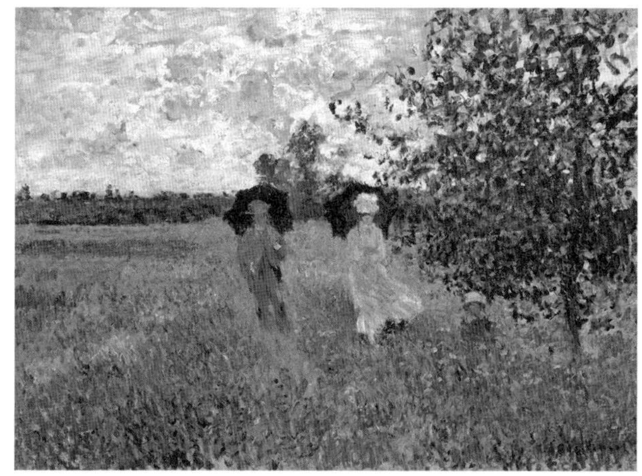

Taking a Walk near Argenteuil, 1875
Oil on canvas, 61 × 81.4 cm
Paris, Musée Marmottan Monet

13 | *Impression, Sunrise*

This painting – Monet's most famous work, since the term "Impressionism" was coined based on its title – depicts a view of the port of Le Havre, with its ships, cranes and factory chimneys. The colours recreate the ephemeral illumination of sunrise, when the sky, the mist, the reflections of the water are impregnated with a pinkish light. The composition brings together all the ingredients that would make Impressionism a precursor style: a modern subject, a landscape that seems barely sketched, painted outdoors, dry brushstrokes, blurred effects, colours that are juxtaposed without being mixed beforehand on the painter's palette. The painting finally reveals what would be Monet's essential research: the luminous perception of the atmosphere surrounding beings and things at a given moment.

14 | *The Bridge at Argenteuil*

In 1874, Monet painted the Argenteuil road bridge seven times, and the railway bridge over the Seine four times. One can see the mastery with which he creates a contrast between the flow of the river, expressed by small horizontal touches, and the mass of the bridge and its piers, amplified by its reflections in the water. By using this iron architectural structure as a motif, Monet aspired to become a painter of modern life, without attempting to erase the new reality of the suburbs.

15 | *The Studio Boat on the Seine*

"A fair wind brought me just enough money, all in one go, to buy myself a boat and have a little wooden cabin built on it, just big enough to set up my easel in." From his boat moored on the Seine, near his home in Argenteuil, Monet can now enjoy unprecedented views of the river, boats and walkers, and observe the subtle metamorphoses of the water up close.

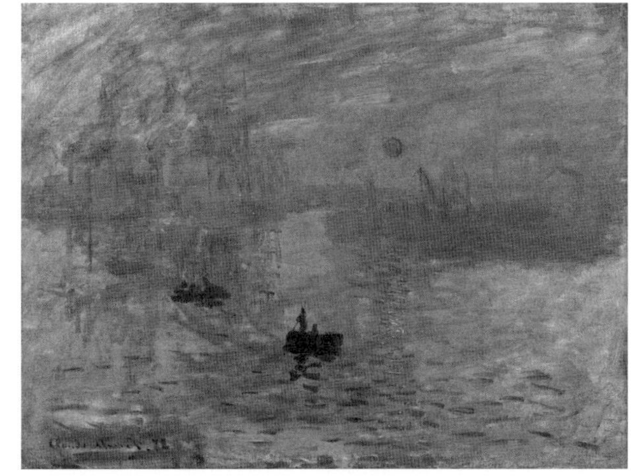

Impression, Sunrise, 1872
Oil on canvas, 50 × 65 cm
Paris, Musée Marmottan Monet

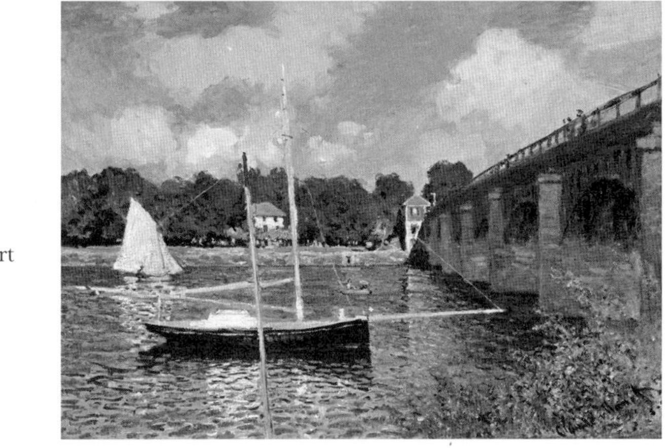

The Bridge at Argenteuil, 1874
Oil on canvas, 60 × 79.7 cm
Washington, The National Gallery of Art

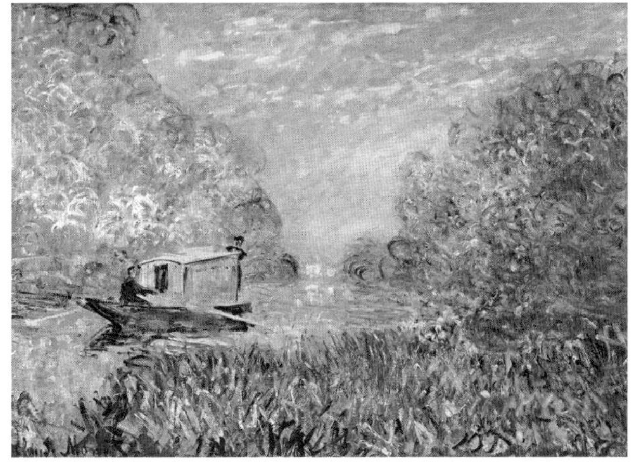

The Studio Boat on the Seine, 1875
Oil on canvas, 55 × 74 cm
Private collection

16 | ***The Parc Monceau***

In 1876, Monet took an interest in the gardens of Paris: among other locations, he painted the Tuileries gardens, encased between various buildings, and produced several views of the Parc Monceau. In this one, he used an extraordinary range of greens, with the shadow of a tree cast on the grass in the foreground. The walkers' silhouettes appear to be literally absorbed by the surrounding greenery.

17 | ***Gare Saint-Lazare***

"[Monet] has exhibited this year some superb interiors of the railway station. One can hear the roaring of the trains which are swallowed up in the overflowing smoke rolling under the vast hangars." In 1877, Émile Zola was struck by the noisy, lively impression of life that emanates from Monet's Gare Saint-Lazare series. This atmosphere was rendered even more accurately, since the artist was allowed to set up his easel inside the railway station itself, where he devoted a dozen paintings to this motif. More than the geometry of the metal architecture, and more than the detailed description of the machines or the travellers, the colourful and luminous effects catch the eye.

18–19 | ***Rue Saint-Denis and Rue Montorgueil***

Monet, a fervent proponent of the French Republic, dedicated two paintings to the 30th of June 1878, the first bank holidays since France's defeat in the 1870 war against Prussia, which also celebrated the opening of the Universal Exhibition in Paris. Flags displayed on occasion of this patriotic demonstration flutter in the wind in the sunshine. The artist successfully captured even the rumour and agitation of the crowd, using vigorous brushstrokes.

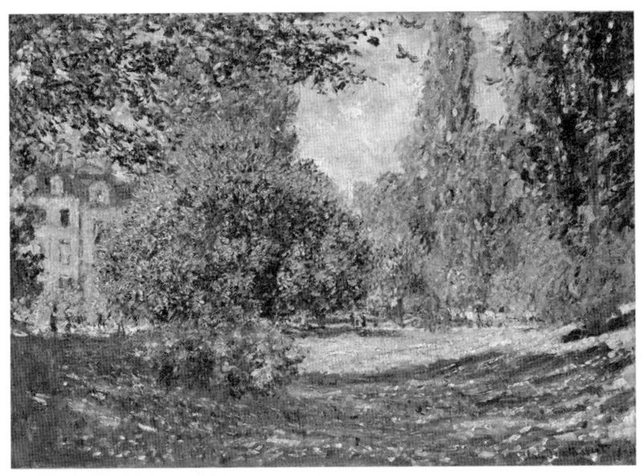

The Parc Monceau
Oil on canvas, 59.7 × 82.6 cm,
New York, The Metropolitan
Museum of Art

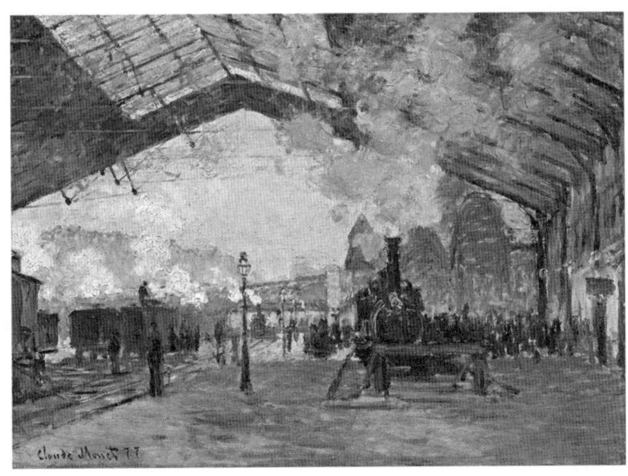

Gare Saint-Lazare, 1877
Oil on canvas, 60.3 × 80.2 cm
Chicago, The Art Institute

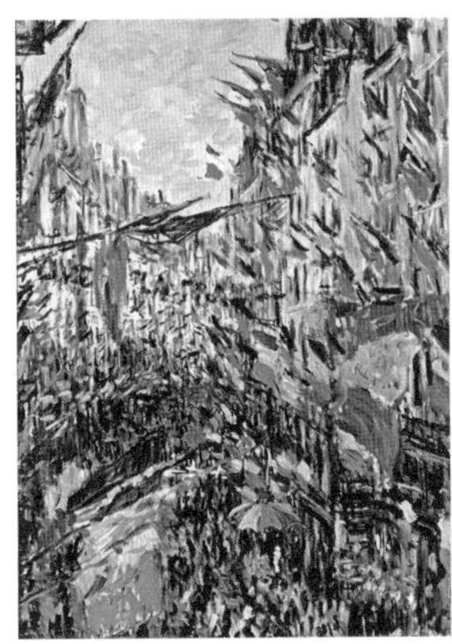

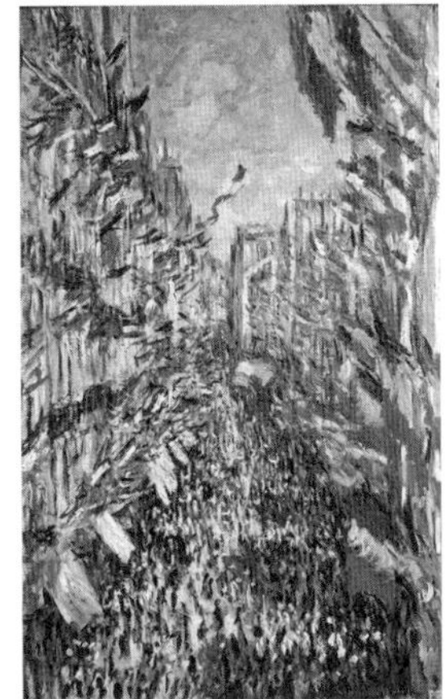

On the left
Rue Saint-Denis, 1878
Oil on canvas, 74 × 52 cm
Rouen, Musée des Beaux-Arts

On the right
Rue Montorgueil, 1878
Oil on canvas, 80 × 50 cm
Paris, Musée d'Orsay

20 | *Sunset on the Seine at Lavacourt, Winter Effect*

Located on the other bank of the Seine, opposite Vétheuil, where Monet settled in 1878, the village of Lavacourt was the subject of two paintings presented to the Salon: the first one, rather conventional, was accepted by the jury, but this one, in which the artist indulges in his pictorial research, was rejected. The misty, cold atmosphere is suggested by fluid brushstrokes, while the riverbanks are rendered using broad brushstrokes and impasto. The balanced composition, featuring a central orange sun, is strongly reminiscent of the famous Impression, Sunrise (no. 13).

21 | *Frost*

To capture "the transitory, the fugitive, the contingent," according to Charles Baudelaire's definition of modernity, such was Monet's task when he painted the metamorphosis of landscapes according to the seasons or the hour of the day. This work depicts the frosty countryside near Vétheuil, delicately suggested by tones of pink, grey and pale blue, barely interrupted by the brown alignment of the bare trees.

22 | *Ice Floes*

"There was a terrible debacle here, and naturally, I tried to recreate it," Monet wrote on 8 January 1880 to his friend the doctor Georges de Bellio. The spectacle captivated the painter to the extent that he produced several compositions of it, using different perspectives, always with the Seine in the foreground. Here, we can see that he applies varied brushstroke effects, differentiating the reflections of the water from the hard blocks of ice, whose shiny facets catch and reflect the light.

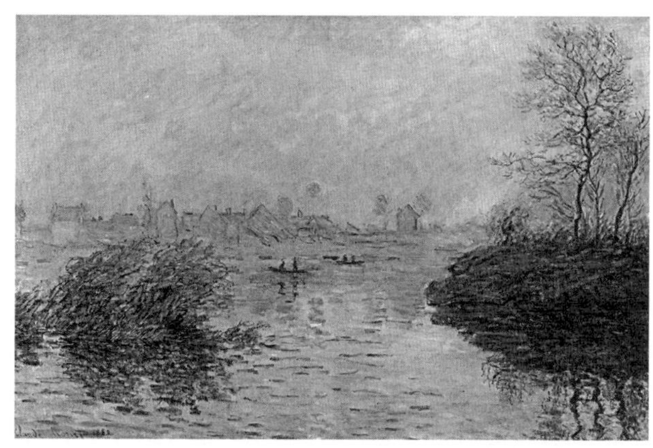

Sunset on the Seine at Lavacourt, Winter Effect, 1880
Oil on canvas, 101.5 × 150 cm
Paris, Petit Palais – City of Paris' Museum of Fine Arts

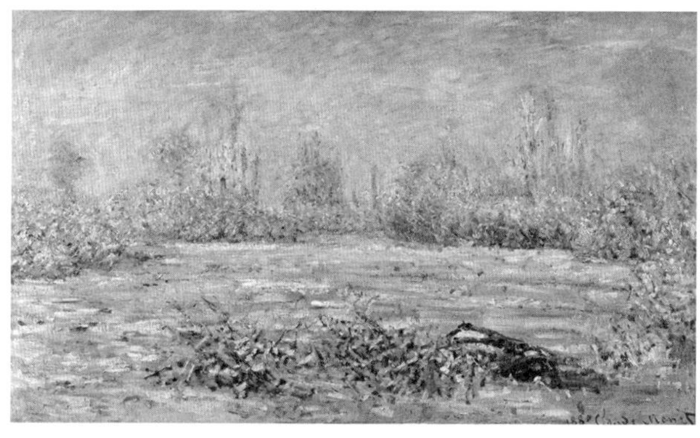

Frost, 1880
Oil on canvas, 60.5 × 99.5 cm
Paris, Musée d'Orsay

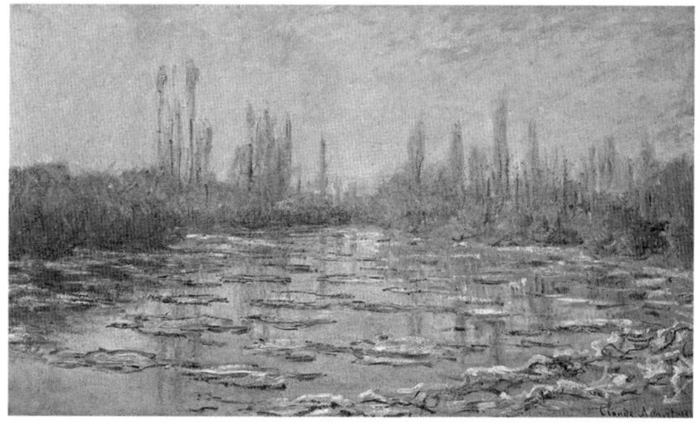

Ice Floes, 1880
Oil on canvas, 60.5 × 99.5 cm
Paris, Musée d'Orsay

23–24| *Rough Weather at Étretat and Morning at Étretat*

In the 1870s, the Normandy coastline had become one of Monet's outdoor studios; he would evoke its mild climes in the manner of Boudin. Ten years later, following in Courbet's footsteps, he sought to suggest its harshness by painting the English Channel's steep cliffs. Using the same perspective, looking down on the beach at Étretat, Monet recreates the location's atmospheric variations: stormy weather, an almost empty beach and a calm, clear morning, allowing fishermen to set out to sea. The use of vertiginous perspectives is a recurring feature in Monet's seaside paintings of this period, in Fécamp, Pourville, Varengeville, and later, in Étretat. Breaking with the tradition of landscape painting, this choice of perspective allowed him to produce a kind of visual shock around the opposition of up and down, emptiness and presence, but also to underline the frailty of man facing the immensity of nature. At the time, the press were not misled when they highlighted the artist's "absolutely remarkable perspective effects."

25| *The Cliff Walk at Pourville*

"The countryside is very beautiful, and I only regret not coming here sooner … One could not stand closer to the sea than I do now, on the very pebbles, and the waves beat against the foundations of the house." Monet wrote these enthusiastic words to Alice Hoschedé in February 1882, just after settling in Pourville. For two years already, the painter had been thrilled to rediscover the seascapes of his childhood. He would spend an increasing amount of time in Normandy until 1886, producing a considerable number of paintings on Pourville, Varengeville, Étretat, their beaches and cliffs, their sky and their horizon.

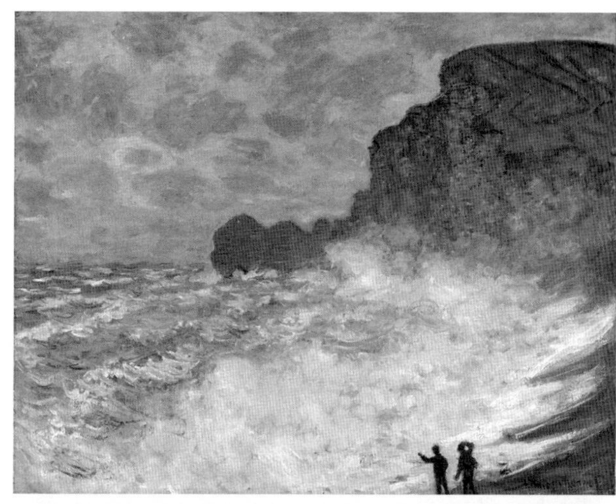

Rough Weather at Étretat, 1883
Oil on canvas, 65 × 81 cm
Melbourne, National Gallery of Victoria

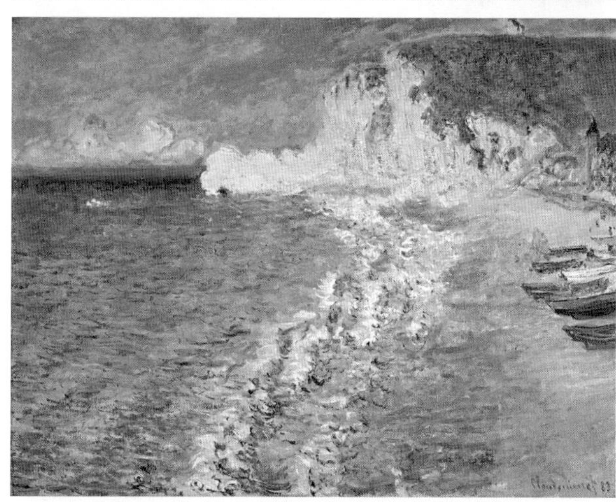

Morning at Étretat, 1883
Oil on canvas, 63 × 81 cm
Private collection

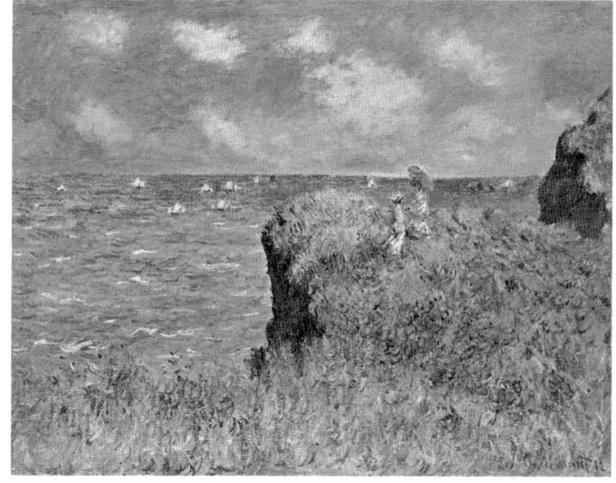

The Cliff Walk at Pourville, Pourville, 1882
Oil on canvas, 66.5 × 82.3 cm
Chicago, The Art Institute

26 | *The Cliffs at Étretat*

Driven by a certain nostalgia, Monet returned to the coastline of Normandy in the early 1880s, where he revisited landscapes that he had captured some fifteen years earlier. In Étretat, he tirelessly worked on the same motifs, circling the cliffs and changing his perspective. When necessary, he would even descend the steep rocks or use a boat to move as close as possible to the subjects that caught his eye. Sometimes, one is bathed in the clear atmosphere of spring, while other times, a storm looms over the roiling water. Boats, silhouettes of fishermen, sails emerge. Different paintings reveal the same attention granted to atmospheric variations, to the light that colours the waves.

27 | *Bordighera*

In December 1883, in the company of Renoir, Monet discovered the Mediterranean and the beauty of the Ligurian coast. In January, he returned alone to work at Bordighera, a famous seaside resort. He was every bit as amazed by the nature there as he was disconcerted by the violence of the colours, particularly that of the sea. His palette became colourful, vibrant, drenched in Mediterranean sun. It was so unusual, in fact, that Monet made a point of warning his dealer, Paul Durand-Ruel: "This may cause those adverse to blue and pink to scream a little, because this brightness, this enchanting light is what I seek to recreate." However, his concerns would prove unfounded: on his return, his dealer would acquire twenty-one of his paintings, which were met with great success.

28 | *Rocks at Port-Goulphar, Belle-Île*

Monet was thrilled by the sight of the rocks of Belle-Île, in 1886: "I find myself in a superbly savage land," he wrote to his friend Gustave Caillebotte. The artist, who wished to paint the Atlantic, would discover extremely harsh motifs, particularly those of violent storms on the coast. The weather is calm, in this view of Port-Goulphar. A deep, dense sea fills the foreground, while the imposing silhouette of the rocks obscures the horizon. This stay in Brittany encouraged the artist to renew his approach of painting. To recreate the vibration of the marine atmosphere, he would use intense colours – blues, greens and violets, applied in varied, flat and wide strokes, or rounded, sometimes forming commas, and often showing agitation. His style differed deeply from his Norman period, as it adapted to the power of its motifs.

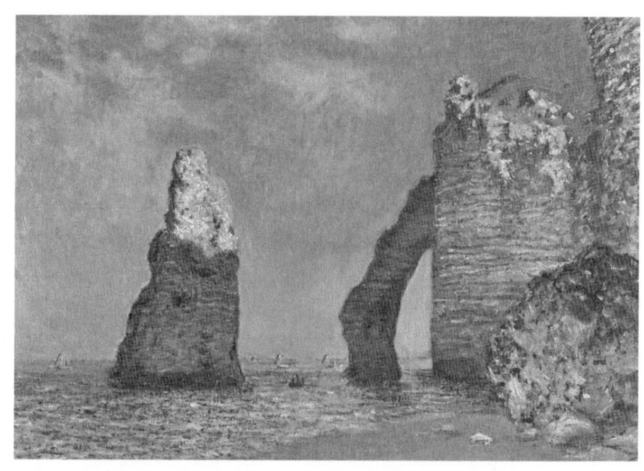

The Cliffs at Étretat, 1885
Oil on canvas, 65.1 × 81.3 cm
Williamstown, The Clark Art Institute

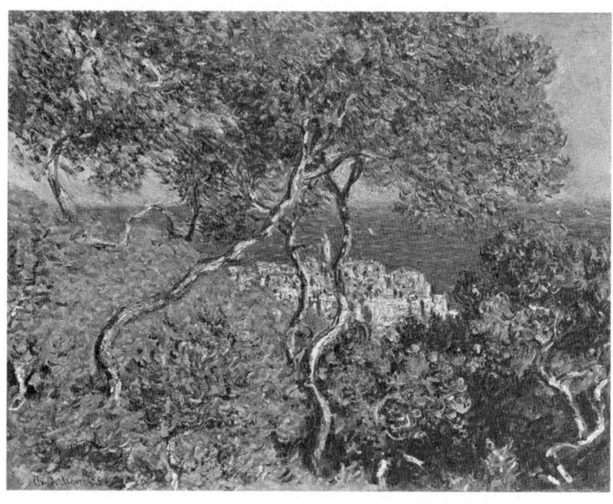

Bordighera, 1884
Oil on canvas, 65 × 80.8 cm
Chicago, The Art Institute

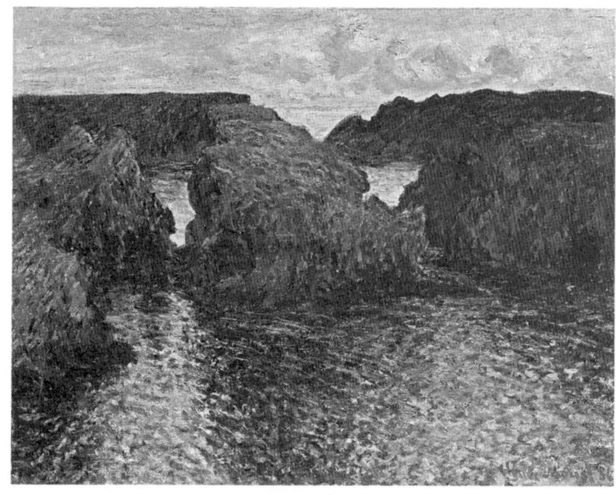

Rocks in Port-Goulphar, Belle-Île,
Oil on canvas, 66 × 81.8 cm
Chicago, The Art Institute

29–30 | *Studies of figures outdoors*

After abandoning the study of figures in the open air, Monet returned to them in 1886, for the last time, with this pair of paintings depicting a woman with a parasol. He treated this theme as a landscape artist, focusing on the envelope of light surrounding the character. Instantaneousness remains his mode of vision: the movement of the dress, the fluttering scarf and the gently curved grass suggest the breeze that was blowing in that moment, while the parasol allows for the distribution of light and shadow. The apparent spontaneity of the scene is, in fact, the result of many hours of posing for the model. In this case, it was Suzanne Hoschedé, the daughter of Monet's companion Alice.

31–32 | *Poplars and Poplars, End of Autumn*

During the 1890s, Monet studied various motifs, whose chromatic and luminous variations form a number of series. The Poplars series, painted between the Haystacks and the Cathedrals, comprises over twenty paintings, in an almost identical format. This row of poplars was located near Monet's house in Giverny, on a bend in the river Epte. Most of these works were painted on a boat or in the immediate vicinity of the riverbank, producing the impression of a low-angle view. In some of them, only three trees appear; in others, seven, depending on how close the artist was to his motif. The rows of trees, the leaves blowing in the wind and the serpentine movement that animates the composition grace these paintings with a particularly decorative character, explaining this series' immediate success.

33 | *Haystacks (End of Summer)*

Until 1890, one could not really state that Monet was producing "series," but rather collections of works on the same subject, attempting to capture variations in atmosphere and light. However, his approach became more radical over the years: motifs gradually lost their importance, giving way to the depiction of ephemeral phenomena caused by light. This journey led to a very banal motif, the haystack, his first real series: twenty or so Haystacks painted from the end of summer to winter, and throughout the day, with the same framing. And to better compare the effects of light on the shapes, the painter chose an identical canvas format, which allowed him to work on them simultaneously and to move from one to another depending on the time of day.

On the left
Studies of figures outdoors:
Woman with a Parasol Facing Right, 1886
Oil on canvas, 130.5 × 89.3 cm
Paris, Musée d'Orsay

On the right
Studies of figures outdoors:
Woman with a Parasol Facing left, 1886
Oil on canvas, 131 × 88.7 cm
Paris, Musée d'Orsay

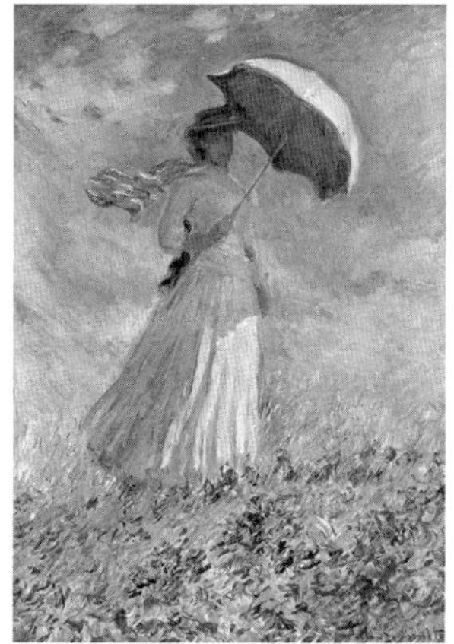

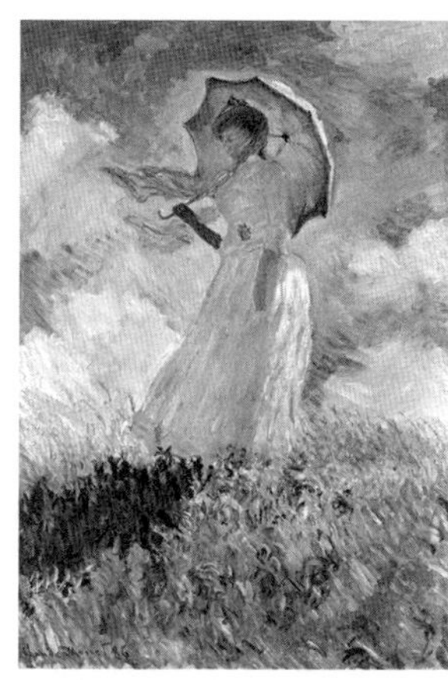

On the left
Poplars, 1891
Oil on canvas, 106.7 × 65 cm
Private collection

On the right
Poplars, End of Autumn, 1891
Oil on canvas, 100.3 × 65 cm
Philadelphia, Philadelphia Museum of Art

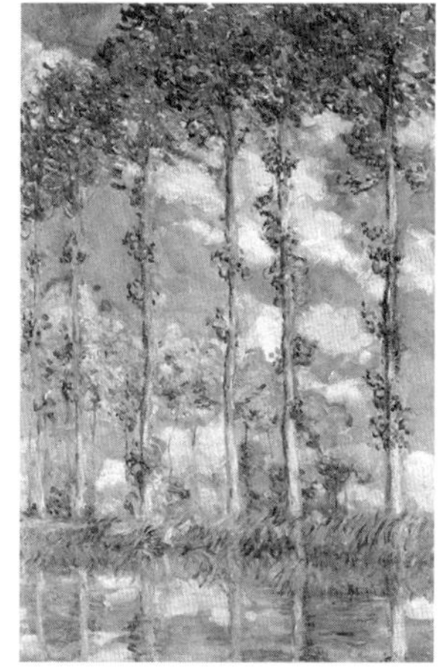

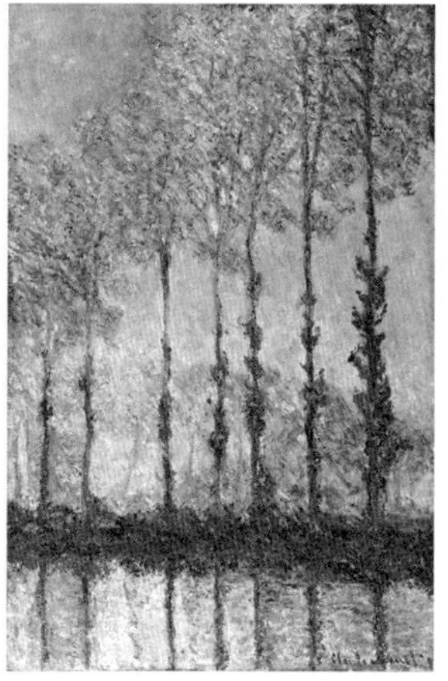

Haystacks (End of Summer), 1890–1891
Oil on canvas, 60 × 100.5 cm
Chicago, The Art Institute

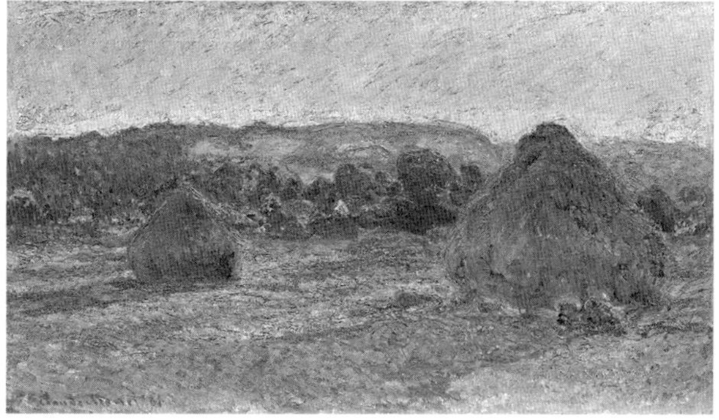

34 | ***Sunrise and Seine near Giverny***

Monet produced the Mornings on the Seine series in the summers of 1896 and 1897. Early in the morning, sitting on his boat, Monet would set about capturing the subtle variations in the atmosphere from dawn to sunrise. In this deserted corner of nature, only trees, water, sky and light appear in blended hues. For a long time, the artist had been fascinated by the effects of mist and fog, which obscure the architectonics of nature and required him to use an almost monochromatic palette, with minute nuances. In these works, Monet recreates the feeling of being enveloped in steam, of hovering above the water.

35 | ***The Boat at Giverny***

Monet's passion for canoeing spread to his family, and in 1887, his daughters-in-law, Suzanne and Blanche Hoschedé, posed as models for a series of works dedicated to boats on the river. In this horizonless painting, the play of reflections prefigures the artist's studies of water lilies.

36 | ***The Customs House at Varengeville***

In 1897, Monet dedicated a dozen paintings to the former customs post at Petit-Ailly, not far from Varengeville. While the perspective differs, their structure is quite identical: working from the heights, the artist produced a bird's-eye view of the small house, located on a rocky spur overlooking the sea, while the sky is reduced to a narrow band.

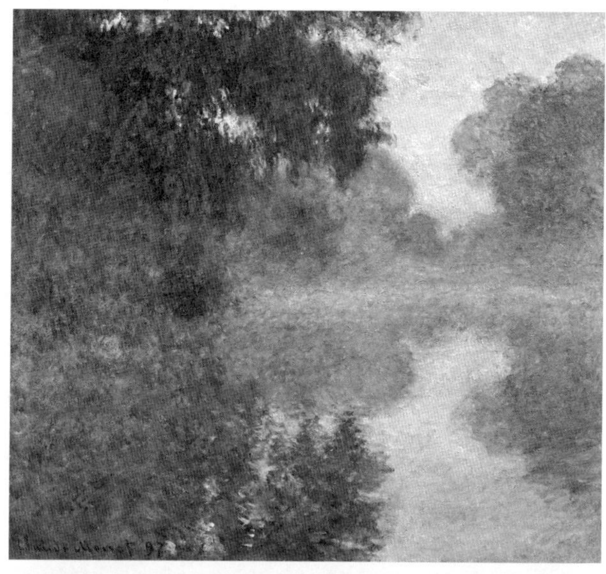

Sunrise and Seine near Giverny, 1897
Oil on canvas, 91 × 93 cm
Paris, Musée Marmottan Monet

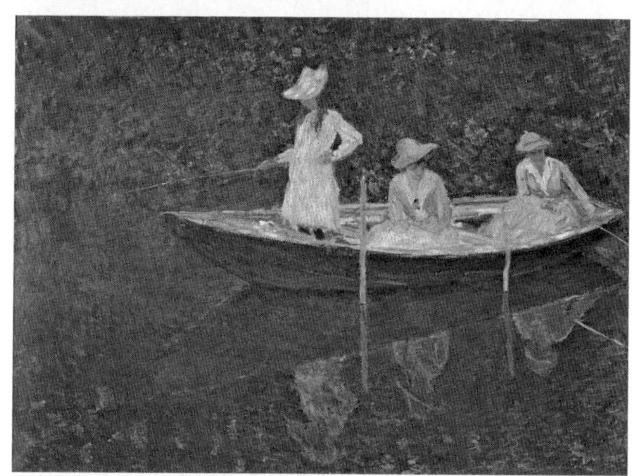

The Boat at Giverny, ca. 1887
Oil on canvas, 97.5 × 130.5 cm
Paris, Musée d'Orsay

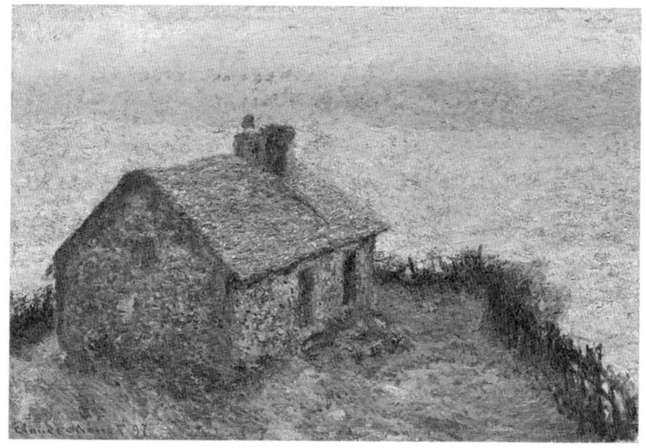

The Customs House at Varengeville, 1897
Oil on canvas, 65.6 × 92.8 cm
Chicago, The Art Institute

37–38 | *The Portal of Rouen Cathedral in Morning Light and Rouen Cathedral, the Façade in Sunlight*

The production of series became a systematic process for Monet when he depicted the western façade of the Rouen cathedral, painted over two periods in 1892 and 1893, from February to mid-April, from three slightly different locations. He would then rework these paintings in the studio. The artist's letters to his wife reveal information on his relentlessness to work on this motif: "[...] I struggle and I work [...], setting my paintings aside, then resuming work on them as the weather changes." This series, the most important of all in terms of numbers – comprising some thirty versions, produced in a nearly uniform format – offers the most spectacular demonstration of Monet's desire to translate variations in the atmosphere and changes in lighting based on one same motif. Depicting the monument from almost the same angle, the series highlights the way shapes change according to the light's evolution. To suggest his subject's matter, the painter used a rough style, which recreates the stone's vibration: "Everything changes, even stone," Monet would write.

39 | *Houses of Parliament*

As Monet returned to the past, he sojourned in London in 1899 and the following two years, where he resumed work on a motif painted in 1871: the Houses of Parliament. This time, however, the study would be carried out in the now systematic form of the series. The location from which he observed the scene, at the end of the day, was a terrace of St. Thomas's Hospital, located on the opposite bank of the river, near Westminster Bridge. But whether under the effect of the sun, a stormy sky or in the fog, the silhouette of the monument remains unreal, like an apparition. Here, the stone architecture seems to have lost all consistency. Sky and water are depicted in homogeneous tones, while brushstrokes are fragmented into multiple coloured patches to convey the density of the misty atmosphere.

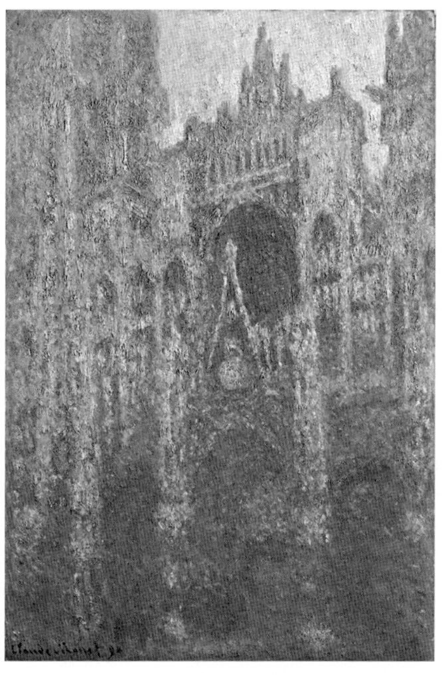

The Portal of Rouen Cathedral in Morning Light, 1894
Oil on canvas, 100.3 × 65.1 cm
Los Angeles, The J. Paul Getty Museum

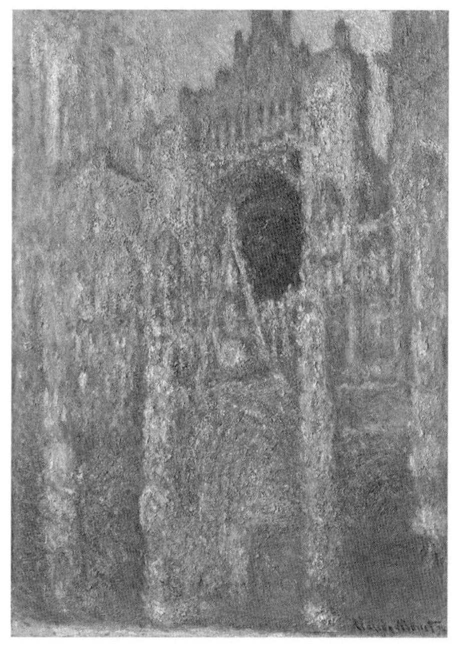

Rouen Cathedral, the Façade in Sunlight, 1892–1894 Oil on canvas, 106.7 × 73.7 cm
Williamstown, The Clark Art Institute

Houses of Parliament, 1900–1903
Oil on canvas, 81.2 × 92.8 cm
Chicago, The Art Institute

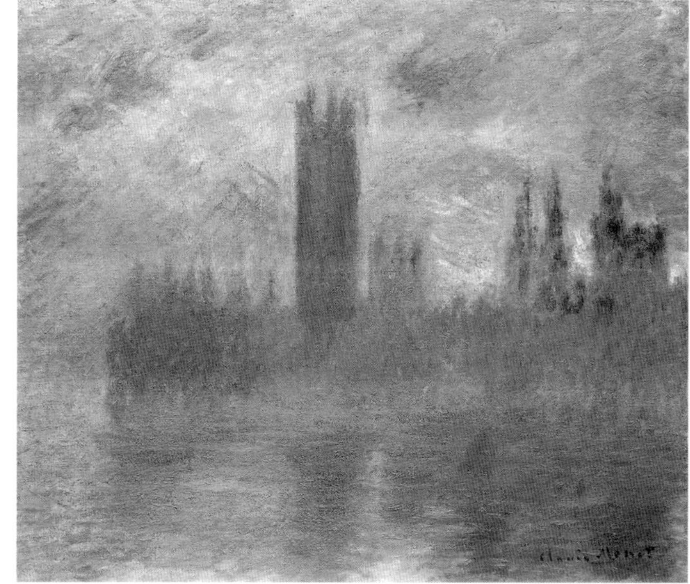

40 | *Palazzo da Mula in Venice*

Venice, in the autumn of 1908, was a discovery for Monet. Painting the Serenissima was a challenge, after Turner and many others had captured it. It was "too beautiful to be painted," said the artist as he arrived. However, he quickly set to work and, sitting in a gondola, began several series of motifs (the Doge's Palace, the Grand Canal, San Giorgio Maggiore) where no human presence appears, while tight framing suppresses the sky. This is the case in this painting of a palazzo on the island of Murano: the façade and the mooring posts lose all materiality in the vibrations of the pink and blue light.

41 | *Garden Path at Giverny*

Purchased in 1890, the property in Giverny became a magnificent estate over the years, embellished by flowerbeds where a professional gardener worked under Monet's orders. This painting wonderfully reproduces the dense vegetation and the profusion of colours. The path leading to the staircase, lined with nasturtiums, serves as the pretext for a clever play of shadows and light.

42 | *Monet's Garden at Giverny*

The entire canvas is invaded by touches of colour, reflecting the abundance of flowers in full season. The light is centred on the clump of irises that forms a mossy mass between the two alleys, while the vertical tree trunks in the background create a rhythm within the composition.

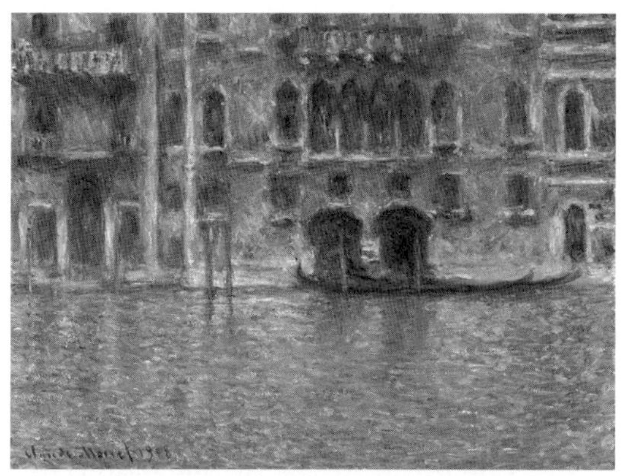

Palazzo da Mula in Venice, 1908
Oil on canvas, 61.4 × 80.5 cm
Washington, The National Gallery of Art

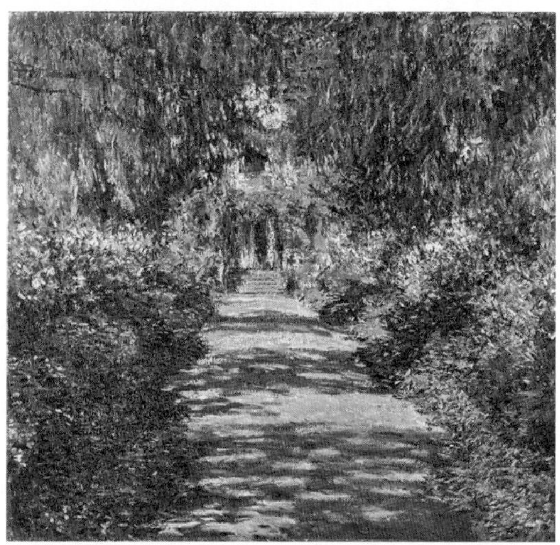

Garden Path at Giverny, 1902
Oil on canvas, 89.5 × 92.3 cm
Vienna, Österreichische Galerie Belvedere

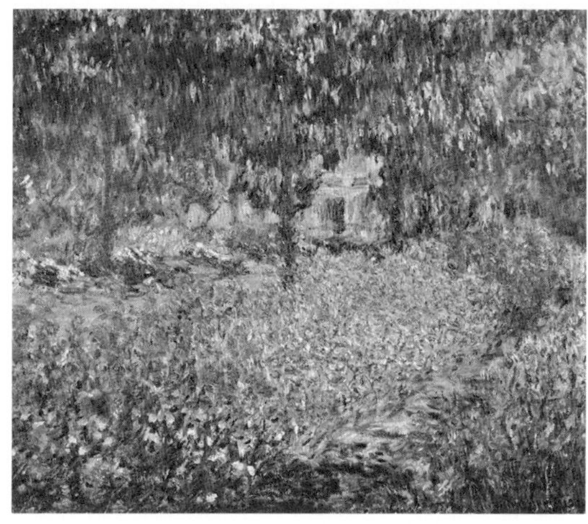

Monet's Garden at Giverny, 1900
Oil on canvas, 81.6 × 92.6 cm
Paris, Musée d'Orsay

43 | *The Water Lily Pond, Green Harmony*

In 1893, Monet obtained permission to have a pond dug in a newly acquired plot of land that extended his garden. He planted water lilies and built a Japanese bridge, seemingly inspired by Hokusai. This reference to Japanese art is hardly surprising, as the artist had been a passionate collector of prints since the 1870s; he even boasted that he was responsible for the wave of Japonism that swept across France in the last quarter of the 19th century. The motif of the bridge would inspire him to produce some twenty paintings in almost square format, featuring more or less close-up views (no. 45).

44 | *Water Lilies*

The "water garden" that Monet created in 1893 would become the sole object of his work for over thirty years. A few years after this landscaping work, the artist produced a first set of paintings featuring only the water lilies and the sky's reflection in the water. From this liquid and moving surface, corolla-shaped flowers emerge amidst the rounded leaves, depicted in a rather realistic way. All spatial reference points are suppressed in favour of a close-up view, giving the illusion of an unlimited surface, of which the painting is only a fragment.

45 | *The Water Lily Pond*

This painting is part of the set that Monet devoted to the motif of the Japanese bridge crossing over the water lily pond (no. 45), of which only the arch is depicted here. Behind the footbridge, which seems weightless, appear the drooping branches of one of four willows of a particular variety, known as the "Babylon willow," which the artist had planted on the banks of the pond. Their characteristic, undulating shape would frequently appear in later paintings, sometimes schematised to the point of abstraction.

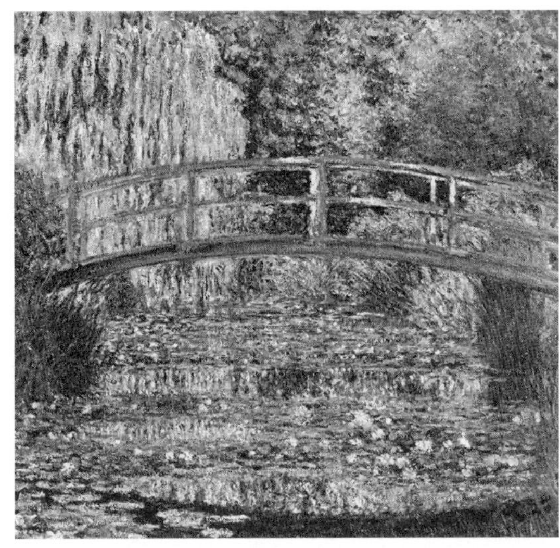

The Water Lily Pond, Green Harmony, 1899
Oil on canvas, 89.5 × 92.5 cm
Paris, Musée d'Orsay

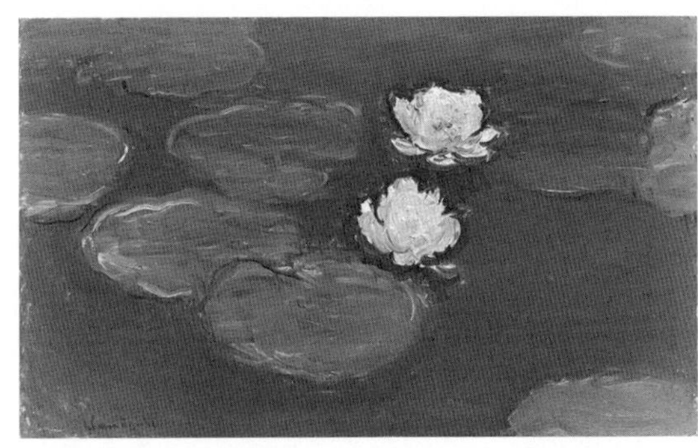

Water Lilies, ca. 1897–1898
Oil on canvas, 66 × 104.14 cm
Los Angeles County Museum of Art

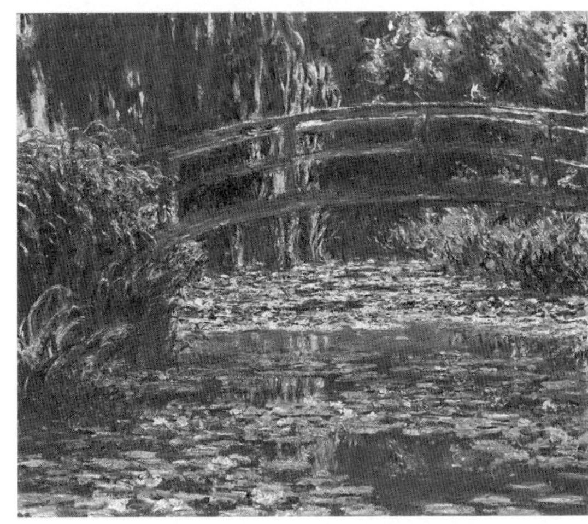

The Water Lily Pond, Oil on canvas,
89.8 × 101 cm
Chicago, The Art Institute

46 | *Water Lilies*

From the 1900s onwards, Monet began a new series, named the "water landscapes." Rather than the motif, what captured his attention was the treatment of space. In this painting, the shoreline has disappeared; only the reflections of the trees bordering the pond can be seen on the surface of the water, in the interstices left by the large patches of water lilies. This was also an opportunity for the artist to display great virtuosity when rendering harmonies of blue, violet and green, punctuated by the white and pink notes of aquatic flowers.

47 | *Water Lilies, Evening Effect*

The unfolding of the hours and their translation by light on the motif are a constant in Monet's work, which also applies to the tightly framed views of his "water garden" (no. 44) and allows him to vary their tones – blue, on this canvas painted at dusk. It appears that the highly decorative nature of these variations which, in a way, form fragments of a larger whole, stirred the artist's mind at the time, creating the idea of a vast circular mural decoration. However, Monet would not undertake this ambitious project before 1914, when it found its final form in the Musée de l'Orangerie.

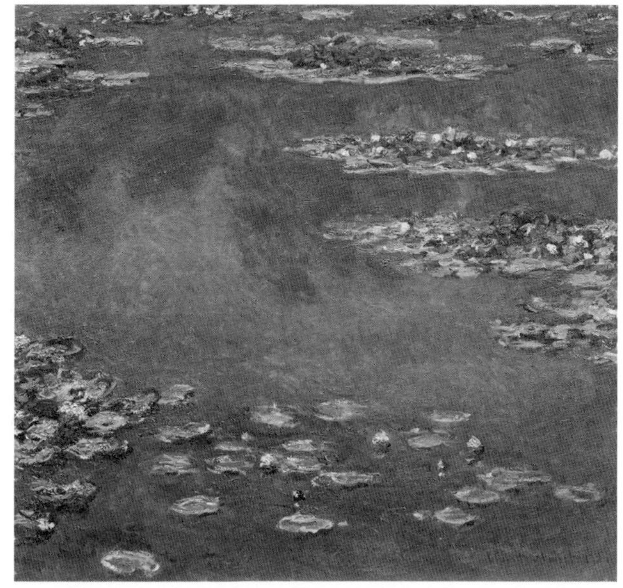

Water Lilies, 1906
Oil on canvas, 89.9 × 94.1 cm
Chicago, The Art Institute

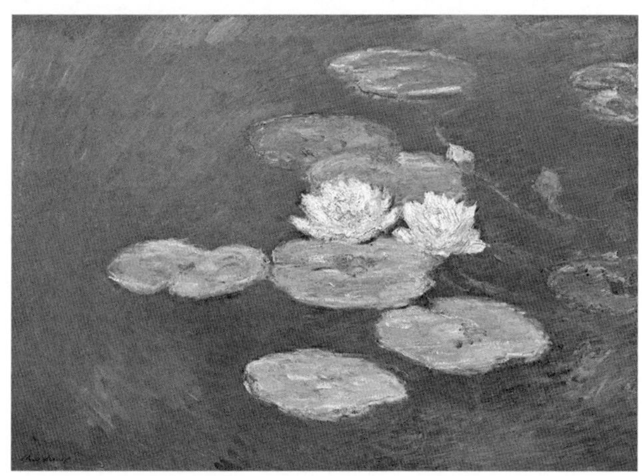

Water Lilies, Evening Effect,
Oil on canvas, 73 × 100 cm
Paris, Musée Marmottan Monet

48–49 | *Water Lilies: Clear Morning with Willows (detail) and Water Lilies: Green Harmony (detail)*

These paintings are part of the eight compositions, on twenty-two panels, destined to occupy the two oval rooms devoted to the Water Lilies in the Parisian Musée de l'Orangerie. They are all of equal height, but varying widths, to accommodate the premises' curved walls. The entire set was fully thought out by the artist, who planned the shapes, the volumes, the layout, the scansion and the spaces between the different panels; Monet even accounted for the natural zenithal light that adds vibrancy to the surface of the canvases, according to the weather. It was during the war of 1914 that this project began to take shape; despite his advanced age, Monet wanted to "undertake great things" and, as a committed patriot, to offer them to the State to celebrate the armistice. The donation of his decorative panels was made official in 1920, but the artist, ever unsatisfied, continued to work on them until his death in 1926. The installation would finally be inaugurated the following year, in the presence of his old friend, the former president of the Council of Paris, Georges Clemenceau, who actively contributed to the implementation of this project.

50 | *Water Lilies*

The freedom of expression in Monet's works from the 1910s onwards is in part due to the tragedy that he suffered: cataract in both eyes would leave him almost blind. Nevertheless, the perfect knowledge of his motifs allowed him to paint what had become a mental vision, which he translated into a tangle of coloured lines that borders on abstraction.

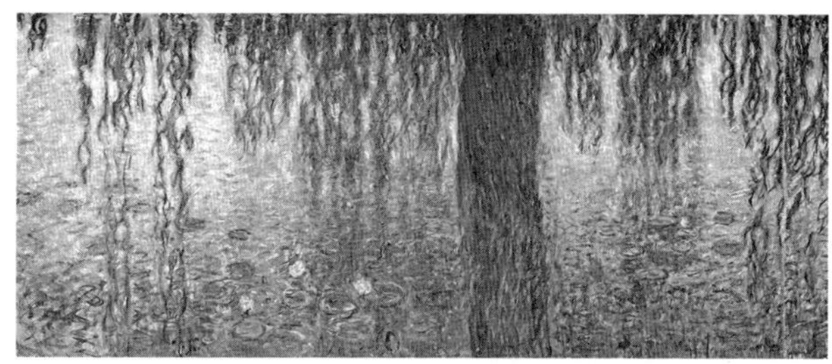

Water Lilies: Clear Morning with Willows (detail), 1915–1926
Oil on canvas, 200 × 1,275 cm
Paris, Musée de l'Orangerie

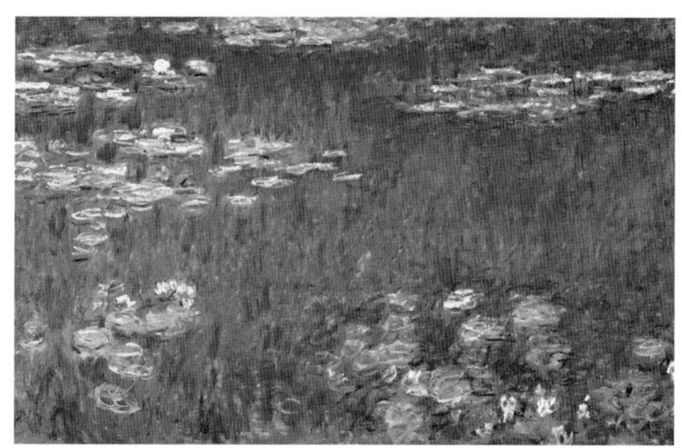

Water Lilies: Green Harmony (detail), 1914–1918
Oil on canvas, 197 × 847 cm
Paris, Musée de l'Orangerie

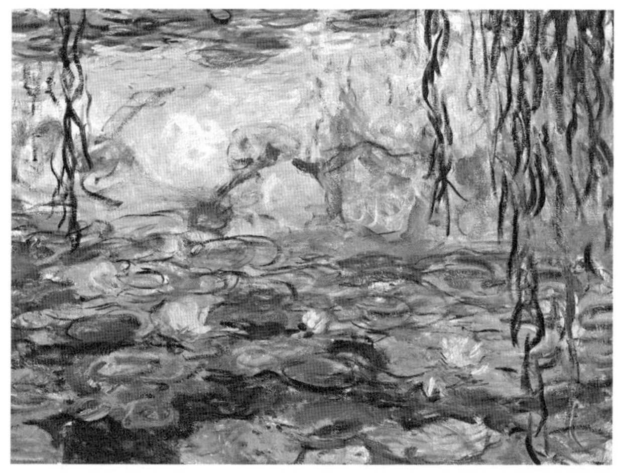

Water Lilies, 1916–1919
Oil on canvas, 150 × 197 cm
Paris, Musée Marmottan Monet

Photographic credits

The numbers refer to those of the images reproduced here.

Baltimore, The Walter Art Museum / © Creative Commons License: 7

Bridgeman Images: 1, 2, 3, 4, 5, 6, 9, 10, 11, 12, 13, 15, 16, 18, 20, 21, 22, 24, 29, 30, 34, 35, 41, 42, 43, 47, 48, 49, 50; / Photo © Christie's Images: 32; / Photo © Luisa Ricciarini: 19; / Bequest of Anne Thomson in memory of her father, Frank Thomson, and her mother, Mary Elizabeth Clarke Thomson, 1954: 31

Chicago, Art Institute of Chicago / Gift of Arthur M. Wood, Sr in memory of Pauline Palmer Wood: 33; / Gift of Mr. and Mrs. Chauncey B. Borland: 28; / Mr and Mrs Lewis Larned Coburn Memorial Collection: 25; / Mr and Mrs Lewis Larned Coburn Memorial Collection: 45; / Mr and Mrs Martin A. Ryerson Collection: 8, 17, 36, 39, 46; / Potter Palmer Collection: 27

Los Angeles County Museum of Art / © Museum Associates/LACMA: 44

Los Angeles, The J. Paul Getty Museum / © Digital image courtesy of the Getty's Open Content Program: 37

Melbourne, National Gallery of Victoria / Felton Bequest, 1913, Public Domain. Digital image © National Gallery of Victoria, Melbourne, 2019: 23

Washington, D.C., National Gallery of Art / Chester Dale Collection: 40; / Collection of Mr and Mrs Paul Mellon: 14

Williamstown, The Clark Art Institute: 26, 38

Creative Commons Zero (CC0) for The Art Institute of Chicago and The Walter Art Museum.

Open Content Program Los Angeles, The J. Paul Getty Museum.

Open Access for Washington, D.C., National Gallery of Art.

© Prestel Verlag, Munich · London · New York, 2023, 3rd edition 2026
A member of Penguin Random House Verlagsgruppe GmbH
Neumarkter Straße 28 · 81673 Munich

produktsicherheit@penguinrandomhouse.de
(The above information is mandatory information according to GPSR and should be used for all queries relating to the safety of our books)

A CIP catalogue record for this book is available from the British Library.

The French original edition was published by Édition Hazan as Monet.

Translation
David Rocher

Proofreading
John Stilwell

Production
Andrea Cobré

Typesetting
Weiß-Freiburg GmbH
Grafik & Buchgestaltung

Repro
Reproscan, Orio al Serio, Italy

Printing and binding
Toppan Leefung Printing

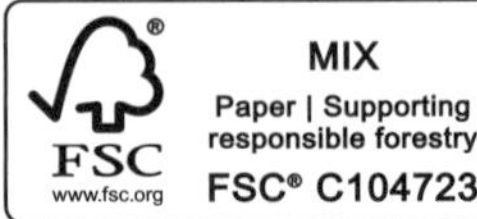

Printed in China

ISBN 978-3-7913-7968-5
www.prestel.com